Flute/ Piccolo

Book One
Beginning

THE BAND METHOD THAT TEACHES MUSIC READING

RHYTHM MASTER

Supplemental Material

By

J.R. McEntyre
Coordinator of Music, Retired
Odessa Public Schools
Odessa, Texas

And

Harry H. Haines
Music Department Chairman
West Texas State University
Canyon, Texas

© Copyright 1992 by Southern Music Company, San Antonio, Texas
International Copyright Secured, All Rights Reserved

Flute Fingering Chart

C   C# Db   D   D# Eb   E

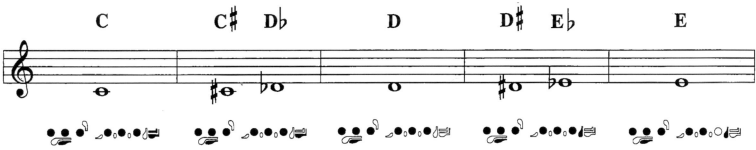

F   F# Gb   G   G# Ab   A

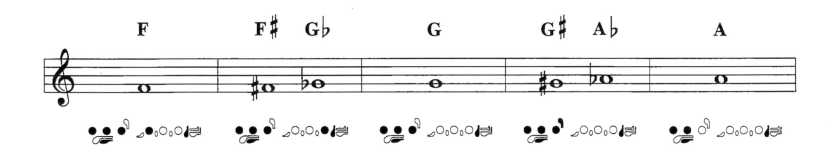

A# Bb   B   C   C# Db   D

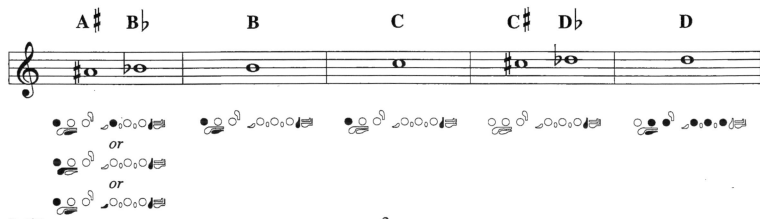

or

or

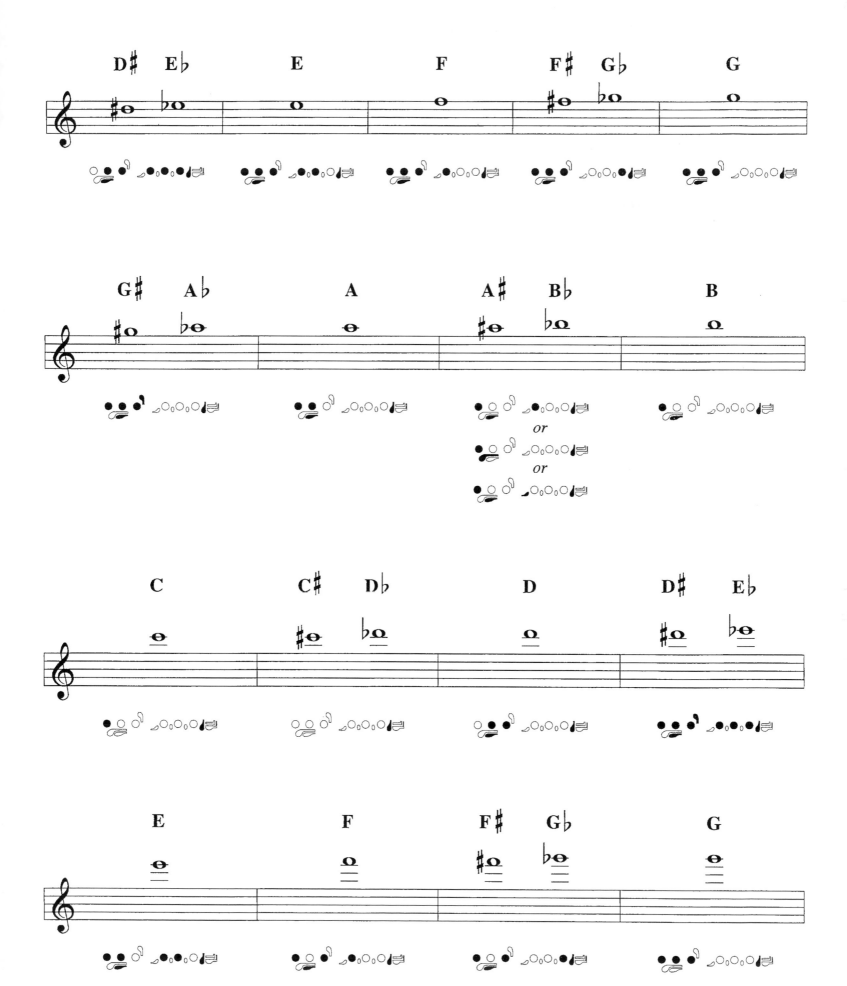

Preliminary Lesson
The Most Important Lesson!

Some aspects of learning to play a band instrument are best learned without an instruction book. This is especially true of the very first stages such as 1) putting the instrument together, 2) learning correct posture and position, and 3) producing the sound. Also, an understanding of a few basic music symbols will be a great help in beginning to read a method book. The authors believe that best results will be achieved if the teacher approaches this lesson using a Suzuki-like presentation. The basis should be rote teaching using much imitation and repetition.

The **Conductor's Guide** contains specific information about each instrument and suggestions from a master teacher for introducing the embouchure.

How long should you spend on a **Preliminary Lesson**? Teaching situations vary but most successful beginning band classes we know get better results when they spend four or five hours on this material. At a minimum, tone production and articulation should be established to a point where students are able to consistently produce the pitch for their first note in **LESSON 1**.

1 Start with the head joint only. Close the end with your right hand and strive to make a big, resonant sound. Then try it open-ended. When you can do this well, try to make a high sound (first closed, then open). Imitate your teacher.

2 Work on correct posture. Pay careful attention to your teacher's instructions. Air is the lifeblood of your sound. No one can play an instrument well unless he/she has good breath support. Good posture is an acquired habit and the time to start is the first day.

3 Put the instrument together properly and learn to hold it correctly. Practice this many times until you can do it well. Instruments may look strong but they are really quite delicate and are easily damaged. Each student must learn how to care for his/her instrument and there will never be a better time than now.

4 Produce a characteristic sound. To do this requires much repetition. Every person learns to play an instrument by the "trial and error" method. One of the essential aspects of success is to "try" enough times to give the method a chance for learning to occur. Repetition, correct instruction, and constant, intelligent analysis are the three primary aspects of learning to play an instrument. The most important of these is (you guessed it) _repetition_! You must go over and over your basic sound always trying to make it better.

5 Practice articulation. Start the sound with your tongue and release with your breath. Learning how to begin and end a tone and coordinate the use of your tongue should be a major goal of this **Preliminary Lesson**.

6 Finally, every student must learn a few basic music symbols before he/she can begin to read music. **LESSON 1** will be much easier if you know the musical terms below. Throughout this book, the red, numbered flags refer to the **Index of Musical Terms** found on the back cover.

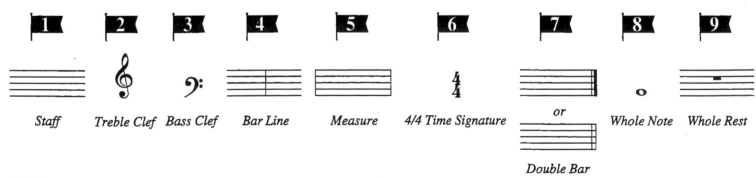

| Staff | Treble Clef | Bass Clef | Bar Line | Measure | 4/4 Time Signature | Double Bar | Whole Note | Whole Rest |

LESSON 1
The First Note

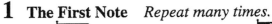

NEW — These "flag" symbols indicate something new. New notes are flagged as "NEW."

1 — A numbered flag refers to the **Index of Musical Terms** on the back cover.

1 The First Note *Repeat many times.*

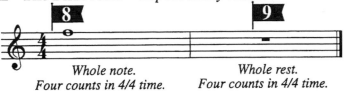

Whole note.
Four counts in 4/4 time.

Whole rest.
Four counts in 4/4 time.

Good tone quality requires good breath support. You cannot become an outstanding player unless you have a supported sound.

2 Whole Notes and Whole Rests *Count each line carefully. Count the rests silently.*

3 Quarter Notes and Quarter Rests

4 Mixing It Up

5 Half Notes and Half Rests

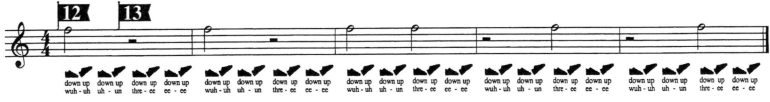

6 All Kinds of Notes

7 All Kinds of Rests *Write the counting on the lines below the staff.*

 *flat*

LESSON 2
The Second Note

Tap your foot, count, and play every line.

8 **The Second Note**   *Repeat many times.*

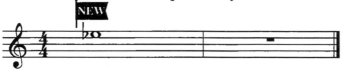

9 **Practice the New Note**

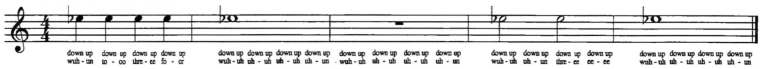

10 **Two-Note Song**   *Write the counting on the lines below the staff.*

11 **First Duet**

12 **Duet Part**

13 **Quarter Notes and Quarter Rests**

14 **All Kinds of Notes**

15 **Who Will Play in the Rest?**

SUGGESTION: Start every class using Warm-up #1 on the inside of the front cover.

LESSON 3
Three Notes

Good players can read music. Remember to tap your foot, count, and play every line.

16 The Third Note   *Repeat many times.*

17 Three-Note Exercise

| down up | down up | down up | down up | down up | down up | down up | down up | down up | down up | down up | down up | down up | down up | down up | down up |
| wuh - uh | uh - un | three - ee | ee - ee | wuh - uh | uh - un | three - ee | ee - ee | wuh - uh | uh - un | three - ee | uh - un | wuh - uh | uh - uh | uh - uh | uh - un |

18 Echo Song

solo   **15**   class   solo   class   solo   class   solo   everyone

19 Duet: Hand Clappers

20 Duet: Finger Snappers

21 All Kinds of Notes

22 Who Will Play in the Rest (Again)?

23 Our First Song

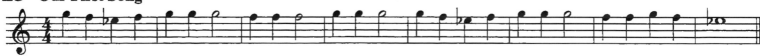

LESSON 4
The Eighth Note Lesson

Always carry your instrument
case with the lid toward you.

24 Introducing Eighth Notes

25 Eighth Notes and Quarter Notes   *Write the counting on the lines below the staff.*

26 Sneaky Second Count

27 Tricky Third Count

28 Freaky Fourth Count

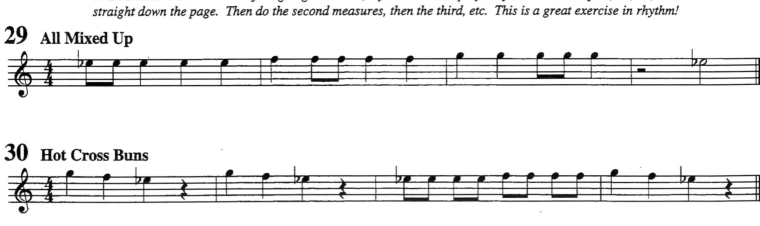

SPECIAL ASSIGNMENT: Before going to line 29, try to count and play the first measures of 25, 26, 27, and 28 straight down the page. Then do the second measures, then the third, etc. This is a great exercise in rhythm!

29 All Mixed Up

30 Hot Cross Buns

31 Merrily We Speed Along

LESSON 5
The Fourth Note/Dotted Half Note Lesson

A dot after a note adds one half the value of that note.

LESSON 6
The 2/4 Lesson

41 **The Most Famous Note**   *Repeat many times.*

42 **Trumpet "Kick" Note**   *Repeat many times.*

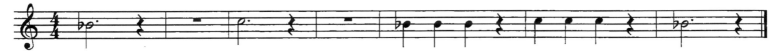

43 **Back and Forth**

44 **Solo Line**

45 **Class Line**

46 **Introducing 2/4 Time**

47 **Grand Ole Duke of York**   *The hardest line in the book so far!*

48 **Twinkle Twinkle**   *Ask your director why there is no double bar here!*

SUGGESTION: Expand your warm-up to include Warm-up #2 (and play it from memory).

Rhythm Set #1
Eighth, Quarter, Half, and Whole Note Rhythms

LESSON 7
The 3/4 Lesson

Good players are known for tone quality.
Are you playing with a supported sound?

49 **High Note** *Write the counting on the lines below the staff.*

How many counts?

_____   _____ (_____) _____

50 **Building Range**
Go back to the beginning of this line.

51 **Eighth Note Etude**
Go back to the first repeat sign.

52 **Variations on Line 51**

53 **Duet: Hand Clappers**

54 **Duet: Knee Slappers**

55 **Blow the Man Down**

56 **Hymn Tune**

LESSON 8
Introducing the Tie

57 Low A Natural *Repeat many times.*

58 Low A Flat *Repeat many times.*

59 Two New Notes

60 Chromatic Woodwinds and High Brass

61 Some Folks Do

62 First and Second Endings

Pop!

63 Mary in a New Key

64 This Old Man

65 Long-Note Challenge *How long can you hold this note? Sneak a breath if you have to.*

66 Brother John round

LESSON 9
The Dotted Quarter Lesson

*Learn how to clean and care
for your instrument properly.*

67 **Introducing the Dotted Quarter and Eighth Rest**

Eighth notes are sometimes written with a single flag on the stem.

68 **Another Way (To Introduce the Dotted Quarter and Eighth Rest)**

69 **Dotted Quarters Everywhere**

70 **Song with Dotted Quarter**

71 **America**

72 **Alma Mater**

73 **Careless Love**

SUGGESTION: Add the first two measures of Warm-up #3 to your daily routine.

Rhythm Set #2
Dotted Quarter Rhythms

LESSON 10
Dotted Quarter Drill

You can tell how good players are by the way they look. Good players have good posture and instrument position.

74 A Lower Note

75 Low-Note Drill

76 Dotted Quarter Drill

77 Hand Clappers

78 Knee Slappers

79 Goin' Home

80 All through the Night

81 Crazy Rhythm Bridge

82 Duet Part

LESSON 11
The Slur Lesson

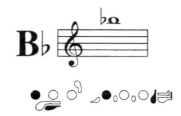

Many people confuse a slur and a tie. How are they different?

83 Slurring Smoothly

84 Dedicated to Clarinets

85 Dedicated to Everyone Else

86 High and Low Notes

87 French Song (with Pick-up Notes)

How do you count the first two notes?

88 Sweetly Sings the Donkey (Round)

double bar

89 Aura Lee

Congratulations! You're half-way through the book!

LESSON 12
Building the Chalameau

90 **Clarinet Teeth-Rattler**

Are you playing with good hand position?

NEW NEW NEW

31 *common time signature*

91 **E Flat Scale**

92 **E Flat Scale Drill**

93 **Hymn Tune in 2/4 Time**

94 **Jingle Bells**

95 **Jolly Ole St. Nick**

96 **Finger Snappers**

97 **Hand Clappers**

Supplementary Lesson
Flute Vibrato

Look up any unfamiliar notes in the
Fingering Chart on pages 2 and 3.

Vibrato, a rapid, slight variation in pitch, is considered an essential part of the characteristic tone of the flute. It is not difficult to learn but, like all other aspects of developing a mature and beautiful sound, must be studied and practiced. The authors of this book suggest the following exercises (in three stages) for developing and refining vibrato:

Stage One: Developing a Measured Vibrato

Say or sing a long note for several seconds. Next, say or sing the long note again adding a number of "uhs" into the sound. Help each "uh" with some extra push with the breath. Strive for a continuous sound, not one which starts and stops with each "uh." Now try to play a long note on your instrument adding the "uhs" to produce a slight variation in the sound. Technically the "uh," or vibrato, is caused by the glottis with some help from the diaphragm. In the beginning, the vibrato effect will have to be exaggerated. Play a concert B flat scale in half notes at ♩=50. Play the scale four times as follows:

First time, play with two vibrato pulses per beat (four on each note)

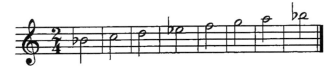

Second time, play with three vibrato pulses per beat (six on each note)

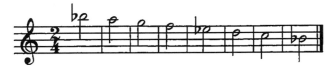

Third time, play with four vibrato pulses per beat (eight on each note)

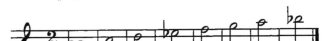

Fourth time, play with six vibrato pulses per beat (twelve on each note)

Stage Two: Developing a Controlled Variation of the Speed

An important aspect of learning to play with vibrato is being able to vary the speed. A vibrato which can only be produced at one speed is no vibrato. Use the following exercise to practice vibrato-like sounds from slow to fast to slow:

Play each note of a B flat scale for fourteen counts at ♩=50. On counts one and two, play two vibrato pulses per beat. On counts three and four, play three vibrato pulses per beat. On counts five and six, play four vibrato pulses per beat. On counts seven and eight, play six vibrato pulses per beat. On counts nine and ten, play four vibrato pulses per beat. On counts eleven and twelve, play three vibrato pulses per beat. On counts thirteen and fourteen, play two vibrato pulses per beat. Think of this long note and the number of vibratos as follows:

Stage Three: Playing with a Free Vibrato

Hold each note three to five seconds, as indicated by the fermata (index, #41). Try to play each note with a free vibrato. Help the vibrato by varying the loudness. Try playing soft to loud to soft on each note. As you increase and decrease volume, let the vibrato grow and ebb both in speed and amplitude.

One of the best ways to develop vibrato concepts is to listen to professional artists. Analyze recordings and live performances. Here are a few "tips" to help you along:

1 The average vibrato in mid-range at medium dynamic has been found to be about five vibrations per second.

2 Notes which are peaks in the phrase, in the high range, or loud usually require a faster vibrato.

3 Low register and/or soft playing usually requires a lighter vibrato (smaller amplitude and perhaps slower).

4 Avoid the following vibrato cliches:
   (a) nanny-goat vibrato (too fast, too narrow)
   (b) bathtub vibrato (too slow, too wide)
   (c) electronic organ vibrato (rigid, always the same speed and amplitude)

LESSON 13
Clarinet High Register

To make a good slur, keep the breath flowing.

98 "The" Scale

99 Clarinets' Line

100 Clarinets Higher

101 Clarinets Higher Still

102 Barcarolle

103 Barcarolle Again *Dedicated to clarinets.*

104 One More Song

SUGGESTION: Gradually add all of Warm-up #3 to your daily routine.

B-497

20

LESSON 14
Introducing Dynamics

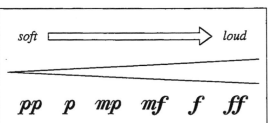

To get a good tone you
must blow very fast air.

105 **Loud Etude**

106 **Soft Exercise** *Does this sound familiar?*

107 **Swing Low**

108 **Mexican Song**

109 **Duet: Part One**

110 **Duet: Part Two**

111 **Clarinets Can't Play This Now - Maybe Later?**

LESSON 15
The Key Signature Lesson

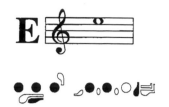

A note "out of key" is a wrong note.

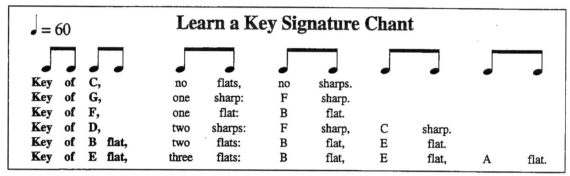

Later, your director will perhaps give you a specific chant for each line.

112 Yankee Doodle with Key Signature

113 Same Song, Different Key

114 Mary Ann

115 Etude in Three Keys

Key of E flat, three flats: B flat, E flat, A flat.   *Key of B flat, two flats: B flat, E flat.*   *Key of F, one flat: B flat.*

LESSON 16
The Cut-Time Lesson

A great deal of music is written in cut-time. Composers like it because it is less work to write.

All successful players are rhythmically independent.

You must be able to play your part while others perform different music.

123 Variations on "Sol-La-Ti-Do"

Variation 1

Variation 2

Variation 3

Variation 4

Variation 5

124 Oom-Pa

23 *afterbeat*

125 Duet Part

126 John Jacob Jingle

Solo

f

"Pa"

mp

"Oom"

mp

Solo

"Pa"

"Oom"

B-497

24

LESSON 18
Syncopation

Always play up-beat notes exactly on the up-beat, not early.

127 Syncopation

128 Syncopation Exercise

129 Our Boys Will Shine (Shortened Version)

130 Camptown Races *Where are the syncopated notes?*

131 Mixed-Up McDonald

132 Tom Dooley

133 Accompaniment

LESSON 19
Building Rhythmic Independence

134 Counting Syncopation

135 Syncopation in Cut-Time

136 Good Night, Ladies

137 Dem Bones

138 March for Hand-Clappers, Knee-Slappers, Finger-Snappers, and Foot-Stompers

A. Hand-Clappers

B. Knee-Slappers

C. Finger-Snappers

D. Foot-Stompers

Optional Supplementary Rhythm Set
Sixteenth Notes

3/8 and 6/8 (Compound) Time

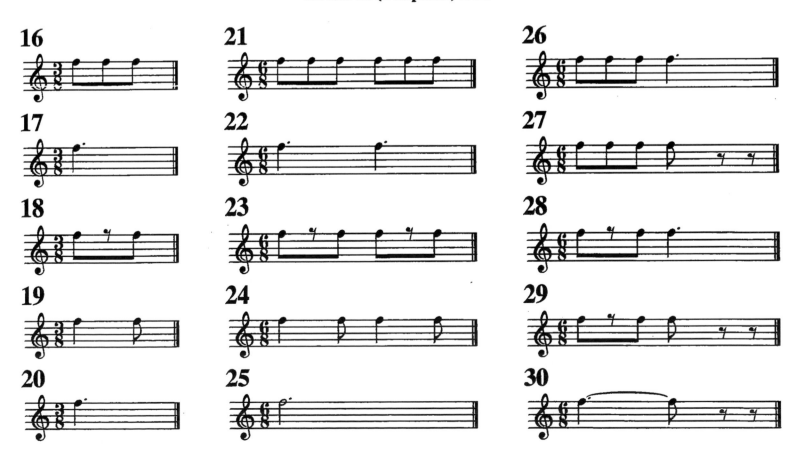

Optional Supplementary Lesson #1
Sixteenth Notes

A Scale with Sixteenth Notes

B Bird

C Polly Wolly Doodle

D Ring-a-Ding-a-Ding

E Scale with Two Sixteenths

F Skip to My Lou

Optional Supplementary Lesson #2
6/8 and 3/8 Time

A 6/8 Scale

B Piano Duet

C Duet Part

D Farmer Song

Watch out!

E Southern Roses Waltz in 3/8 Time

F Hymn Song

G Lovely Evening Round

Special Songs for Individual Practice

Look up any unfamiliar notes in the
Fingering Chart *on pages 2 and 3.*

Special Songs for Individual Practice

Look up any unfamiliar notes in the
Fingering Chart *on pages 2 and 3.*

Reuben and Rachel

Eency Weency Spider

Scales to Prepare for Book Two

F Concert Major Scale

E Flat Concert Major Scale

B Flat Concert Major Scale

B Flat Concert Chromatic Scale

Traditional "One And" Counting System*

Most teachers of band instruments agree that the teaching of music reading can be done most efficiently and effectively with a counting system. A rhythmic vocabulary helps communication and promotes understanding. It doesn't seem to matter which counting system is used as long as there is a system and it is used consistently. Two suggested counting systems are offered on these two pages.

The idea of saying the "number" of the count on which a note occurs and saying the word, "and," for any note that occurs half-way after the beat has been used for many years. The basic idea with many variations can be found in hundreds of music books. Probably the most widely circulated publication using this system of counting is the *Haskell Harr Drum Method*. Because of its long history (published in 1937 and still used today), its expansive use, and the general public perception that percussionists are supposedly experts at counting, many band directors have adapted a counting system that is remarkably similar. The following is a somewhat modified summary of "one and" counting that might be used by teachers and students for this band method:

I. Notes of One or More Counts

For notes of one count (or longer), simply say the number of the count on which the note begins and continue counting for the duration of the note. Thus, a note which receives one count and which begins on the first beat of the measure would be counted, "one." If the note occurs on the second count say, "two," etc. A note of longer value would simply be counted longer. The following example quickly illustrates the counting system as applied to rhythms (including rests) of one, two, three, or four counts:

II. Counting the Sub-divisions

Notes which receive less than a whole count and which are divisible by two (some would say simple time) are counted as follows:

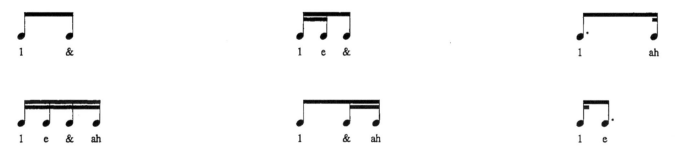

Notes which receive less than a whole count and which are divisible by three (some would say compound time) are counted as follows:

*For a complete explanation of this counting system, see *the Haskell Harr Drum Method*, published by M. M. Cole Publishing Company.

Eastman Counting System*

While there is no "official" counting system endorsed by the Eastman School of Music, there was a system written by Alan I. McHose which was published in his series of theory texts. Because he was a theory instructor at the Eastman School for many years and his books were used as textbooks for his theory classes, most Eastman students of the 1940s, 50s, and 60s used his counting syllables.

For almost a third of a century these graduates of one of America's largest and most highly regarded music schools have been doing a great deal of "evangelizing" about their counting system. Many have been leaders in music education and their teaching techniques have been widely copied. The authors of this band method, neither of whom attended the Eastman School, have adapted the system and used a modified version in teaching beginning band classes. Both recommend its use with this band method.

I. Notes of One or More Counts

Notes of one count (or longer) are counted much the same way as in any other counting system. One major difference is that notes longer than one count are held with a continuous word-sound. Thus, a whole note in 4/4 time would be counted, "onnnnnnnnnne," for four counts. The following example quickly illustrates the counting system as applied to rhythms (including rests) of one, two, three, or four counts:

II. Counting the Sub-divisions

Notes which receive less than a whole count are categorized into rhythms which are divisible by two or those which are divisible by three (some would say duple and triple rhythms). Again, any note which occurs on a downbeat is simply counted with the number of the count. The important difference is that a note which occurs on the last half of a count is counted, "te," (Latin, rhymes with May) and notes which occur on the second or third fraction of the count are counted, "lah," and, "lee." Everything else is counted, "ta" (pronounced, "tah").

Rhythms Which are Divisible by Two (Read Down)   Rhythms Which are Divisible by Three (Read Down)

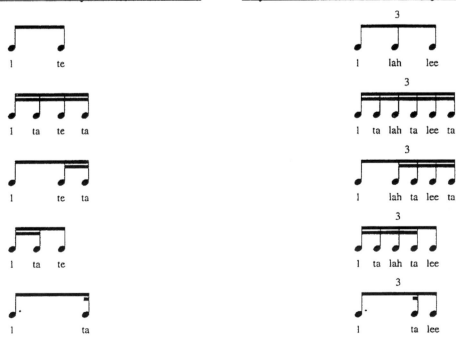

*For a complete explanation of this counting system, see the *Ear Training and Sight Singing Dictation Manual*, published by Prentice Hall.

Warm-ups

Play a good, strong tone.

Look up any unfamiliar notes in the
Fingering Chart *on pages 2 and 3.*

Warm-up #1

Warm-up #2

Warm-up #3

Warm-up #4

Practice Record Chart

Week	Day 1	Day 2	Day 3	Day 4	Day 5	Day 6	Day 7	Total Time	Parent's Initials	Weekly Grade
1										
2										
3										
4										
5										
6										
7										
8										
9										
10										
11										
12										
13										
14										
15										
16										
17										
18										

Week	Day 1	Day 2	Day 3	Day 4	Day 5	Day 6	Day 7	Total Time	Parent's Initials	Weekly Grade
19										
20										
21										
22										
23										
24										
25										
26										
27										
28										
29										
30										
31										
32										
33										
34										
35										
36										

Index of Musical Terms

1 **Staff** - the five lines and four spaces where notes are placed

2 **Treble Clef** - a symbol that indicates which notes are on each line and space of the staff; also called the "G" clef

3 **Bass Clef** - a symbol that indicates which notes are on each line and space of the staff; also called the "F" clef

4 **Bar Line** - divides the staff into measures

5 **Measure** - the space between two bar lines

6 **4/4 Time Signature** - The numeral on top indicates that there are four beats in each measure. The bottom numeral indicates that each quarter note gets one beat.

7 **Double Bar** - marks the end of a section

8 **Whole Note** - gets four beats in any time signature with a 4 as the bottom numeral, such as 4/4 time; equivalent to two half notes

9 **Whole Rest** - gets four beats in any time signature with a 4 as the bottom numeral (except 3/4); equivalent to two half rests

10 **Quarter Note** - gets one beat in any time signature with a 4 as the bottom numeral; equivalent to two eighth notes

11 **Quarter Rest** - gets one beat in any time signature with a 4 as the bottom numeral; equivalent to two eighth rests

12 **Half Note** - gets two beats in any time signature with a 4 as the bottom numeral; equivalent to two quarter notes

13 **Half Rest** - gets two beats in any time signature with a 4 as the bottom numeral; equivalent to two quarter rests

14 **Duet** - a song for two players or two parts

15 **Solo** - means that the part is to be played by one person

16 **Eighth Note** - gets half a beat in any time signature with a 4 as the bottom numeral; equivalent to two sixteenth notes

17 **Dotted Half Note** - gets three beats in any time signature with a 4 as the bottom numeral; equivalent to three quarter notes

18 **Accompaniment** - a part that supports the melody but is subordinate to it

19 **Harmony** - the consonant sounding of two or more notes together

20 **2/4 Time Signature** - two beats in each measure; each quarter note gets one beat.

21 **3/4 Time Signature** - three beats in each measure; each quarter note gets one beat.

22 **Eighth Rest** - gets half a beat in any time signature with a 4 as the bottom numeral

23 **Afterbeat** - a note played on the second half of the beat

24 **Repeat Sign** - means to go back to the beginning of the song or section

25 **Tie** - combines the durations of two notes of the same pitch

26 **First and Second Endings** - play through the first ending, repeat, then skip the first ending and play through the second ending

27 **Round** - music for two or more in which the performers play the same music but start and end at different times

28 **Dotted Quarter Note** - gets one and one half beats in any time signature with a 4 as the bottom numeral; equivalent to three eighth notes

29 **Slur** - a line connecting two or more notes which indicates that only the first note joined by the slur is to be tongued

30 **Pick-up Note/Notes** - the notes in an incomplete measure at the beginning of a song; note values are usually taken from the last measure

31 **Common Time Signature** - the same as 4/4 time

32 **Dynamics** - indicate the relative volume of a note or notes

33 **Key Signature** - sharps or flats placed at the beginning of a section indicating that certain notes are to be sharped or flatted throughout that section

34 **Cut-time** - the same as 2/2 time; two beats in each measure; each half note gets one beat.

35 **Fine** - marks the end of the song

36 **D.C. al Fine** - means to go back to the beginning of the song and play until "Fine" is reached

37 **Syncopation** - an accented note (or stressed note) that comes on an unaccented beat; frequently a note that starts on the up-beat and is held through the next downbeat

38 **Sixteenth Note** - gets one fourth of a beat in any time signature with a 4 as the bottom numeral

39 **6/8 Time Signature** - two beats in each measure; each dotted quarter note gets one beat.

40 **3/8 Time Signature** - one beat in each measure; each dotted quarter note gets one beat.

41 **Fermata** - means to hold the note longer than the indicated value

42 **Flat** - lowers a note one half step

43 **Sharp** - raises a note one half step

44 **Natural** - cancels the effect of a sharp or flat

45 **Repeat Measure** - means to repeat the preceding measure

46 **Double Repeat Measure** - means to repeat the preceding two measures

Selected Flute Publications

METHODS

MEADOR, REBECCA/ MARSHALL, JEAN

| B572 | Preparatory Etudes for Flute | HL3770917 |

COLLECTIONS

EPHROSS, ARTHUR
Ephross, Arthur/ Stark, Jan

| B392CO | Church Instrumentalist, Bk. 1a (Grade 2) | HL3770593 |

KOEHLER/DROUET

| SS246 | Six Sonatinas and Three Duos Concertants (Grade 2) | HL3773854 |

This collection of flute duets includes "Six Sonatinas" Op. 96 by Hans Koehler and "Three Duos Concetants" by LFP Drouet.

VOXMAN, HIMIE/ BLOCK, R.P.

| B490 | Duet Fun, Bk. 1 (Grade 2) | HL3770771 |

SOLO WITH PIANO

BACH, J.S.
Wummer, John

| SS117 | Sonata No. 2 in E-flat (Grade 2) | HL3773717 |

EWAZEN, ERIC

| SU447 | Concerto for Flute (reduction) | HL3776365 |

Written for Julius Baker. Recorded by Marya Martin and Czech Philharmonic Chamber Orchestra for Albany Records.),

HAYDN, FRANZ JOSEPH
Voxman, Himie/ Block, R.P.

| ST759 | Adagio and Rondo (Grade 2) | HL3775567 |

TULL, FISHER

| SS969 | Erato (Grade 2) | HL3774659 |

Erato is a flowing, one movement quasi recitative. It is an ideal recital choice for contemporary music programs.

SOLO WITH GUITAR

FAURE, GABRIEL-URBAIN
Fink, Michael

| ST337 | Sicilienne (Grade 2) | HL3774989 |

DUO

PACHELBEL, JOHANN
Ephross, Arthur

| ST741 | Canon (Grade 2) | HL3775545 |

TRIO

BOISMORTIER, JOSEPH BODIN DE
Voxman, Himie/ Block, R.P.

| ST510 | Gavotte and Two Minuets (Grade 2) | HL3775227 |

MOZART, WOLFGANG AMADEUS
Guenther, Ralph

| SS491 | Allegro (from Divertimento No. 3, K. 229) (Grade 2) | HL3774123 |

This delightful arrangement for intermediate beginner ensembles is based on Mozart's original Divertimento K. 439b (Anh. 229) composed in 1783 for 3 basset horns.

| SS493 | Menuetto (from Divertimento No. 3 K229) (Grade 2) | HL3774125 |

TCHAIKOVSKY, PETER
Guenther, Ralph

| SS745 | Dance Of the Reed Flutes from "The Nutcracker" (Grade 2) | HL3774407 |

Also called "Dance of the Mirlitons", this very recognizable melody is the seventh movement from Tchaikovsky's famous ballet, "The Nutcracker". This arrangement for flute trio by Ralph Guenther makes use of predominantly homophonic writing in the flutes, but also includes an optional piano accompaniment.

QUARTET

SOLOMON, EDWARD

| ST201 | Quatro Giocoso (Grade 2) | HL3774804 |

This playful quartet offers young players an introduction to independent part playing, and is a wonderful selection for either recital or contest.

CHOIR

PACHELBEL, JOHANN
Webb, Robert K.

| ST390 | Canon (Grade 2) | HL3775055 |

Exclusively distributed by HAL•LEONARD® CORPORATION

Questions/ comments? info@laurenkeisermusic.com